Thrust like a right fist into the northwesternmost corner of the contiguous United States, the 6,400-square-mile Olympic Peninsula is a land of marked contrast: dripping coastal rain forests and rain-shadow farmlands, rushing rivers and mirror lakes, ice-carved mountain peaks and glacial lowlands, rugged shoreline and swampy tidal flats. Topographical change and water, in all its forms, define the mood and character of the peninsula. It is bordered on the east by the Hood Canal fjord, on the north by the Strait of Juan de Fuca leading to Puget Sound, and on the west by the Pacific Ocean. The heart of the peninsula is the Olympic Mountains and its life blood the rivers that rush from the highlands to the sea. Turquoise and swollen with glacial melt in spring, limpid and full of reflected color by autumn, the rivers are the links between high country, forest, and coastal ecosystems that make the biological diversity of the peninsula possible.

POCKET PORTFOLIO®
–Number Ten–

OLYMPIC

NATIONAL PARK and PENINSULA

including
OLYMPIC PENINSULA:
A Timeless Refuge
by
NICKY LEACH

SIERRA PRESS
Mariposa, CA

ISBN 0-939365-67-7
ISBN 13: 978-0-939365-67-8

Copyright 1998 by:
Tellurian Press, Inc.
4988 Gold Leaf Drive
Mariposa, CA 95338

PRODUCTION CREDITS

Series Editor-in-Chief: Jeff Nicholas
Book Design: Jeff Nicholas
Essay and Captions: Nicky Leach
Editor: Cynthia Newman Bohn
Photo Editor: Jeff Nicholas
Production Assistant: Laura Bucknall
Printing coordination: TWP America, Inc

Front Cover: The Hall of Mosses, Hoh Rain Forest. ©JEFF D. NICHOLAS
Front Cover Inset: Point of Arches, dawn. ©CHARLES GURCHE
Frontispiece: Sol Duc Falls, Sol Duc River. ©STEVE TERRILL
Title Page: Mount Olympus from Low Divide. ©PAT O'HARA
Back Cover: Blacktail deer on Hurricane Ridge. ©RICHARD D. STRANGE

The publishers would like to take this opportunity to express our
appreciation to the photographers who made their imagery
available for review during the editing of this title. On behalf of
those who will view this book—Thank You!

If you would like to receive a complimentary
catalog of our publications,
please call: (800) 745-2631
e-mail: siepress@yosemite.net
or write: SIERRA PRESS
4988 Gold Leaf Drive, Mariposa, CA 95338

Killer whale petroglyph, Makah culture.

JEFF FOOTT

The Hood Canal Twana (Skokomish), north-shore Klallam, and coastal Queets, Hoh, Makah, Quinault, and Quileute tribes have called the peninsula home for millennia, making full use of abundant salmon; whales, seals, and land-based game; roots and berries; and redcedar and other forest products. Under the watchful gaze of a natural pantheon that included all-powerful Raven and Thunderbird, the tribes alternately warred and traded with one another from Columbia River to Alaska, using ceremonial potlatch celebrations to maintain the power balance. All this changed in 1855, when Washington governor Isaac Stevens signed treaties with all tribes dispossessing them of their lands and forcing them on to tiny reservations where people became disconnected from their cultural traditions. Today, a renaissance of pride and interest in Northwest coastal tribal traditions has occurred, beginning with the discovery, in 1970, of a 450-year-old Makah whaling village entombed by a mudslide. Cedar longhouses and nearly 500,000 artifacts of outstanding beauty and utility were uncovered, perhaps the most important archeological find in North America. They are now on display in the Makah Cultural and Resource Center in Neah Bay.

OLYMPIC PENINSULA:
A Timeless Refuge
Essay by Nicky Leach

"AYE, HE'S REALLY SOMETHING!" whispers the wiry Scotsman, crouched behind his telephoto lens. "The park is beautiful, but this bear is an unexpected bonus. It's really made my day."

The visitor's smile says it all. What good fortune to chance upon a wild black bear this close to Hurricane Ridge Visitor Center. Summer sightings are quite common, but you can't count on seeing bears. Today we are in luck. We sit quietly and watch the show.

It's a beautiful high-country summer's noon. The crystalline air in these nearly 6,000-foot subalpine meadows is buzzing and alive. Bumblebees weave drunkenly from buttercup to buttercup, reminding me of nothing so much as stripe-jerseyed rugby players on a lazy summertime pub crawl in the English countryside. Mosquitoes and flies home in on hiker's sweat like B-52 bombers on a wartime air raid. An unseen Olympic marmot, one of 16 animals endemic to the Olympic Peninsula, whistles an alarm to its colony from a nearby rock, just as a barrel-chested Columbia black-tailed doe and her fawn pass by.

Other hikers arrive, quadriceps quivering from the steep mile-and-a-half climb to the top of Hurricane Hill. To the south, the glacier-clad Olympic Mountain Range, the center of Olympic National Park, forms a jumble of toothy peaks etched against a robin's-egg-blue sky. The grassy meadows, moist with snowmelt and dotted with dark sedimentary rock outcrops, are quilted with swatches of pink heather, purple lupine, milky yarrow and phlox, and threads of orange tiger lily, scarlet Indian paintbrush, and sapphire-hued bellflower. Shadowy valleys cleave into treelined drainages thousands of feet below.

To the north, on this clear day, we can see all the way across the placid waters of the Strait of Juan de Fuca to Vancouver Island. The busy tourist center and harbor of Port Angeles, Washington, sits a few miles below, while metropolitan Seattle bustles a mere 100 miles to the east. Hurricane Hill is truly one of the most scenic picnic spots in the Northwest, but right now neither the scenery nor food is uppermost in anyone's mind.

Spanish explorers and British colonists and traders were the first Europeans to discover the Olympic Coast and to try to lay claim to it for their countries in the late 1770s. They were forced to retreat, though, when local Hoh and Quileute Indians killed the foreign landing parties. The Strait of Juan de Fuca was located by British trader Charles Barkeley in 1787 and reconnoitered the next year by his countryman, John Meares, who named Mount Olympus. Between 1790 and 1792, three Spanish expeditions investigated the coastlines of the Strait of Juan de Fuca, with a Spanish expedition briefly establishing a military post at the entrance to Neah Bay in 1792. That same year, British Captain George Vancouver thoroughly explored the Puget Sound region, while American Captain Robert Gray explored the mouth of the Columbia River. Both claimed the Oregon Country, as it was known, for their respective countries.

The peninsula's accessible lowland forests

Big-leaf maples in the Elwha River Valley.

PAT O'HARA

When Britain gave up its stake in lands below the 49th parallel in 1846, Americans began to settle on former Indian lands along Puget Sound and the Strait of Juan de Fuca. The Olympic interior was a mystery to most of these coastal settlers until 1885, when U.S. Army Lieutenant Joseph O'Neil and his party explored the Hurricane Ridge area above Port Angeles. But before he could carry out a second, more thorough investigation in the summer of 1890, O'Neil was scooped by an expedition mounted by the *Seattle Press* in December 1889. Although the party of six men and four dogs was hampered by winter avalanche dangers, inadequate provisions, and transportation problems, the adventurers made it up the Elwha drainage and down the North Fork of the Quinault, returning the following May to great acclaim. Within a decade, O'Neil and others had surveyed the Olympics and named many peaks, putting to rest rumors that the interior was a hidden Eden containing vast mineral wealth and fierce Indians.

The object of our attention, a full-grown black bear, is about 200 feet away, waking up from a nap beside a glacial cirque lake. As we watch, he lumbers onto all fours and ambles toward a stand of subalpine fir to snack on its pale, tender, new tips. He stands on hind legs and pulls the boughs toward his large snout with surprising deftness for such lethal paws, licking and sucking on the shoots with relish. Standing around six feet tall, three or four feet wide, and weighing up to one-quarter ton, this bear is like a huge, hairy sumo wrestler circling an opponent. His fat quivers as he shambles around the fir. After a 10-week binge diet of shoots, truffles, ants, berries, and other fare, the bear will be ready for the long winter ahead. Even before the deep snows come, around October, he will ease into hibernation in a protected nook and remain there until next June, living off fat stores and recirculating wastes into usable proteins. Right now, everything depends on lunch.

There is nothing so fascinating as witnessing other creatures unselfconsciously going about their business on home turf, and I suddenly realize that this is why I am feeling so happy. I imagine myself part of the bear's world for a while, seeing these fresh mountain meadows through his eyes, walking through the high country with the certain sense of home and power that he feels, trading all my human choices for a life of simpler pleasures and predictable needs. Idle thoughts, the reverie of a summer's day, but isn't that why we love to be in nature, to embrace something normally locked away in our primitive brains? What is it we reconnect to in natural places? Is it a remembrance of animal kinship and the right way to live together in the world? Is it an acknowledgment of how interdependent we all are? We need places like the Olympic Peninsula where we can question what it means to be human; to be a small part of the natural world, not always in charge; and to still feel humbled and a little scared in the face of something larger and stronger than ourselves.

The Bailey Range seen from Hurricane Ridge, winter afternoon.

PAT O'HARA

The profusion of life in the Queets Rain Forest.

WILLIAM NEILL

Gull feather on Rialto Beach.

GEORGE WARD

Seastack off Second Beach, sunset.

JEFF NICHOLAS

The peninsula's accessible lowland forests and shores are a crazy quilt of private and public holdings and eight Indian reservations. Olympic National Forest flanks Olympic National Park on three sides and includes 90,000 acres of designated wilderness. The 1,400-square-mile park, of which 95 percent is designated wilderness, protects the Olympic Mountains, their watersheds, the finest old-growth forests, and more than 62 miles of wilderness coastline. The earliest Olympic Forest Reserve, set aside by President Cleveland in 1897, preserved 2,188,800 acres of the peninsula but was reduced in size by a subsequent administration, leaving old-growth forests open to logging. The seeds of lasting preservation were planted in 1909, when president Theodore Roosevelt created 600,000-acre Mount Olympus National Monument to protect overhunted Roosevelt elk in the upper rain forest valleys. An ideological tug-of-war regarding the fate of the remaining old-growth forests and wildlife led, in 1938, to the setting aside of Olympic National Park, which has been recognized by UNESCO as a Biosphere Reserve and World Heritage Site for its remarkable diversity.

Unrelated to the Cascade volcanoes, the 6,000–8,000-foot Olympics are crumpled sedimentary rocks contained within a horseshoe of harder Crescent Formation basalts, most easily seen on the way to Hurricane Ridge. The basalts oozed up along the ocean floor about 50 million years ago, cooling on contact with the ocean into mountains of "pillow basalts." This new material was joined by marine and continental sediments, which shed into the ocean in such thick layers they eventually compressed into sandstone and shale strata. Meanwhile, the mobile Juan de Fuca Plate and American Plate ground past each other, shoving the expanding Pacific Plate under the continent. In the vicinity of Vancouver Island, though, where North America bends, the oceanic plate got hung up. Offshore basalts crashed into the continent and partially upended, resulting in the massive pile-up of older volcanic and sedimentary rocks that are now known as the Olympic Mountains.

White Mountain seen from near Anderson Glacier.

PAT O'HARA

Gray Wolf Ridge (in distance) and lichen covered rock near Deer Park on Blue Mountain.

PAT O'HARA

TIME PLAYS TRICKS ON YOU HERE, on this large, rain-soaked peninsula, the northwesternmost corner of the continental United States. Could it be that the omnipresent rain and coastal fogs are to blame, or perennially snowclad Mount Olympus? Perhaps it has something to do with the fragrance of redcedar, the glint of a homecoming salmon in a rushing river, the sight of oyster-gatherers on a Hood Canal beach, or the discovery of a little homestead cabin deep on a trail in the heart of wilderness. Maybe it's the way so many places along Highway 101 take on a comforting, moss-between-the-toes look.

Whatever it is, I find myself slowing down and stepping back in time whenever I am here—a most agreeable sensation.

In the heart of the Olympics, the scene seems straight out of the Ice Age: ice-carved peaks rising above the clouds, creaking glaciers, granite boulders rafted here from Canada, scoured valleys, smoothed and striated rocks, mountain cirques, deep gravel moraines deposited in lowland valleys, frigid rivers and lakes turquoise with high-country glacial flour, sounds to the north and east, a fjord separating the Olympic and Kitsap Peninsulas.

And then, to the west, the scene is polar opposite—literally. You could be walking in equatorial America, 65 million years ago, when the climate was as warm and humid as western Africa, dinosaurs ruled the earth, and trees and plants reached gigantic proportions. The 120–167 inches of rain that falls on the west coast Queets, Quinault, and Hoh River Valleys creates perfect conditions for dripping spruce–cedar–big-leaf maple temperate rain forests, some of the best remaining examples of rain forest in the United States. A visiting friend who has experienced both South American jungle and Olympic rain forest observed that the peninsula's temperate rain forests are quieter, greener, and more restful, though no less overgrown than equatorial forests. The big trees, with their record-breaking ages and girths, 30-story heights, and moss-and-lichen-clothed trunks and branches, invoke awe as well as a little magic. She imagines the Green Man watching from the bole of a redcedar. We are, after all, people who are barely out of the woods.

And then there's the Pacific Coast. Booming surf pounds the longest wilderness coastline in America, tossing onto the grey sand piles of enormous stripped logs as pale as tusks in an elephant's graveyard. Offshore sea stacks topped by

During the last ice age, the Olympic Peninsula was covered on all but its west coast and subalpine zones by Canadian glaciers that occupied Puget Sound, the Strait of Juan de Fuca, and Hood Canal. Climatic warming ended the Ice Age roughly 13,000 years ago, but its effects remain: icy, clear, meltwater sounds, lakes, and rivers; craggy peaks; Canadian granite boulder erratics orphaned atop glacially polished cliffs; and thick gravel outwash deposits in lowlands, including a large terminal moraine that backed up Lake Crescent. Fed by deep winter snows, around 266 perennial glaciers still carve pathways down Olympic mountainsides, melting every spring and charging rivers with eroded high-country sediments, gravels, and boulders that scour short, deep drainages to the estuaries. The Brothers, Mount Constance, and the other basaltic peaks of the Olympic horseshoe resist erosion, giving these rocks an etched, rampart-like appearance on the eastern Olympic skyline.

Opposite: Glacially carved Lake Crescent and Storm King Mountain, dusk.
PAT O'HARA

Point of Arches.   ADAM JONES/Dembinsky Photo Associates

windblown spruce materialize out of the fog like wandering sea sages with wild hair. At daybreak, a Quileute Indian fishing boat turns into the tiny harbor of La Push and a curious harbor seal periscopes up to take a look. In the frontyard of someone's weathered home, a carved ceremonial canoe with a thunderbird motif painted on its prow awaits the next tribal paddle to a neighboring Indian fishing village.

Looking out from the coast, it's easy to imagine that nothing lies beyond, and you could sail off the edge of the world. Looking in, how to penetrate the cliffs, dense forests, and rivers to the interior? After a number of ill-fated attempts to explore the coast by Spanish, English, and Russian expeditions, British captain George Vancouver and American trader Robert Gray succeeded in 1792, setting up rival claims to land and waters that had been home to Peninsula Indian tribes and their ancestors for as long as 12,000 years.

Stories have a habit of attaching themselves to a land where everything grows to mythic proportions. Just over a century ago, the Olympic Mountains were still unexplored by Euroamericans. People speculated that a great central plateau concealed Shangri-La and tribes of cannibal Indians. The *Seattle Press* Exploring Expedition of the winter of 1889-1890 was paid to find out. They blazed a north-south crossing of the Olympics, via the Elwha River Valley, which drains much of the northern Olympics, and lived to tell the tale—just. Their real-life exploits, the stuff of a *Boy's Own* comic, made terrific reading. Soon others were drawn into what was once *terra incognita*. A little adventure makes us all feel more alive.

Seastacks in early morning fog, Rialto Beach.

MARILYN KAZMERS/Dembinsky Photo Associates

The misty Olympic coast is one of America's wildest and most remote shorelines. Ebbing and flowing with the tides, freshwater rivers mingle with saltwater here, with some that are adjacent to Indian reservations shielded from storms by walled harbor channels that must be dredged and fortified constantly to keep them navigable. Sheer bluffs covered with wind-pruned Sitka spruce forests overlook sprawling grey-sand beaches strewn with huge kelps and 50-foot peeled log piles tossed ashore by 100 mph winter storms. The sound of wave pounding shore is deafening. Wave erosion leaves behind sandy terraces and characteristic coves, windows, and arches in rocky headlands, which eventually collapse into tree-topped sea stacks. Some of the the rocks at Point of the Arches are particularly interesting. Composed of basaltic, igneous, and sedimentary rocks, they are 144 million years old, more than twice the age of the Olympic Mountains' oldest rocks, and may be the remnants of an earlier North American continent.

Seastars and green sea anemones.

PAT O'HARA

Ruby Creek and Ruby Beach, sunset.

PAT O'HARA

Large sections of the Olympic Peninsula coastal ecosystem are now protected within Olympic National Park, Olympic Coast National Marine Sanctuary, wildlife refuges, and island wilderness. The combination of river mouths, coves, sand and gravel beaches, mild year-round climate, and nutrient-rich offshore waters makes for tremendous natural diversity, helped along by the peninsula's position halfway between the boreal north and temperate south. Gray whales pass along the Pacific coast during spring and fall migrations, while sea otters and harbor seals feed and play among offshore kelp beds. Intertidal pools teem with hidden life—as much as 4,000 creatures per square foot—including colorful seaweeds, mussels, urchins, and anemones. Sea stars and whelks prey on their poolmates, but all become delicacies for gulls, crows, raccoons, bears, and other low-tide beachcombers. The inland coast, with its bays, sand spits, sluggish estuaries, and lapping waters, is quiet by comparison—a haven for orcas and porpoises, as well as cormorants, brant, bald eagles, and other birds.

Blue Glacier below Mount Olympus.   JANIS BURGER

Rhododendron (Washington's State Flower) near the Dosewallips River.   JANIS BURGER

The west side of the Olympic Peninsula is the wettest place in the Lower 48 United States, drenched by as much as 167 inches of annual precipitation, rising to 200 inches atop 7,965-foot Mount Olympus. By stark contrast, an average of 18 inches of rain falls on Sequim, which lies within the famous "rain-shadow" of the Olympics. The peninsula's maritime location and compressed, high-relief topography are key to understanding this huge discrepancy in rainfall. Warm prevailing winds pick up moisture from the Pacific then blow onshore year round, often turning violent in the winter. Warm air is funneled up the steep, forested drainages of the Hoh, Queets, and Quinault river valleys, where it quickly cools and turns to rainfall, then snow on Mount Olympus, less than 10 miles away. By the time air currents reach the other side of the Olympics, little moisture remains. This accounts for the frequent blue skies over the Strait of Juan de Fuca and prairie savannah vegetation of the Dungeness area, associated with a drier climate.

Sunrise over the Strait of Juan de Fuca and Dungeness Spit (Dungeness National Wildlife Refuge).

PAT O'HARA

Big-leaf maples along the Elwha River, winter.

PAT O'HARA

The Dosewallips River, spring run-off.

GEORGE WUERTHNER

Thirteen rivers drop the short distance from Olympic high country to lowland, providing important transportation corridors between marine and freshwater zones. Within the protected headwaters of Olympic National Park, shady riverbanks, fallen logs, boulders, and gravels shelter salamanders, as well as steelhead and coho, Chinook, sockeye, pink, and chum salmon returning upriver to spawn. Once hatched, salmon fry grow in brief safety here readying for the downstream gauntlet to the ocean. After a few years feeding in rich ocean waters, Olympic salmon have reached the record sizes they need to make the difficult return run to upstream spawning grounds, where they die and provide essential nutrients to the greater Olympic ecosystem. Their numbers are diminishing, though. Logging and development have severely reduced native salmon stocks along Hood Canal rivers and threaten other salmon runs. Restoration of at least part of the salmon habitat on the Elwha River seems imminent, however, following 1992 legislation approving removal of two turn-of-the-century dams that block passage of spawning salmon.

YOU CAN FOLLOW IN THE FOOTSTEPS of the *Press* party today by hiking the entire Elwha Trail from Whiskey Bend to the North Fork of the Quinault, 45 miles away. The route goes up and down, takes in homestead cabins and historic ranger stations, and is very popular. Some guidebooks like to boast that even though one should allow a week to hike the trail, it *could* be done in one very long summer day by an exceptionally fit hiker. I can't imagine who would attempt such a thing.

Most of the trails in the Olympics backcountry, all of it designated wilderness, require a high degree of fitness. No roads cross the range, so to see the park interior you must hike on sections of the more than 900 miles of trail that criss-cross the mountains. This is not so bad if you start at a high-country trailhead rather than in one of a number of lowland drainages. Elevation gain or loss is the real kicker here, with the strong possibility of poor weather thrown in for good measure.

My Norwegian friend and I found that out when we decided to hike a section of the trail that drops 5,300 feet from Hurricane Hill to the Elwha River, 7.5 miles away. A good day hike, we thought, and downhill the whole way. Views of Mount Olympus and the Bailey Range were said to be magnificent, and the Elwha River is an attractive destination. The appointed day dawned wet and grey, but we went ahead, setting up camp at Altaire Campground in the Elwha, leaving a car near the quaint CCC-era ranger station, and drove a second vehicle to Hurricane Ridge. Here, in a setting as moody as the Yorkshire Moors in *Wuthering Heights*, we donned rain suits, attached bells to our packs to deter bears and cougars, and set off.

Five hours later, soaked from head to foot, knees spasming, we shuffled to our car at the trailhead in the Elwha, foolish with fatigue but high on achievement. The experience was classic Olympics: incessant rain, heavy fog, teasing glimpses of high, glacier-clad mountains, lush wildflower meadows, silent forest, precipitous trail, and enough obstacles in our path to keep us alert. Only one other pair of hikers passed us all afternoon.

The Olympic Peninsula supports 1,452 species, subspecies, and varieties of native vascular plants, of which eight, including Flett's violet and Piper's bellflower, are endemic, having survived the Ice Age in their high-country biological refuges. Olympic snow mole, Olympic marmot, Olympic chipmunk, Olympic Mazama pocket gopher, and Beardslee and Crescenti trout are also genetically unique, while black bear, cougar, Columbia black-tailed deer, and Roosevelt elk live in other areas of the Northwest. Absent, though, are mammals such as grizzly bear and lynx, which are found across the water in the Cascades; Olympic's red foxes and mountain goats were introduced. At present, the Olympic Peninsula provides sanctuary for nine species federally listed as endangered and threatened, with one, bull trout, a candidate for listing and another 13 Species of Concern. The greater Olympic ecosystem is intact, except for one missing link, the endangered gray wolf, which preys on elk and deer. The possibility of eventually reintroducing wolves to the peninsula, a controversial issue, is now being studied.

Opposite: Blacktail deer in blowing fog. STAN OSOLINSKI

The threatened northern spotted owl.   JANIS BURGER

Biologists monitor the numbers of habitat-dependent species within specific Olympic ecosystems as a measure of overall habitat health: anadramous fish such as salmon in the rivers; heathers and endemic plants in the high country; mollusks in the tidal flats; northern spotted owls in the old-growth forests; and Roosevelt elk herds in the rain forests. Some species, such as threatened marbled murrelets, salmon, and elk, move through several ecosystems, making them particularly vulnerable to habitat disturbances. Timber management practices, marine harvesting, pollution, hunting, introduced species, recreational use, population growth, and encroaching development impact fragile Olympic Peninsula ecosystems and require continual monitoring to balance human needs with those of nature. As in the past, fluctuating weather patterns affect this balance. In recent decades, warm winter El Niño ocean currents from Baja may be occurring more frequently, resulting in changes to the rich marine environment and the animal populations linked to it.

Later, relaxing in camp as dusk fell over the Elwha, I watched a flyfisherman walk out into the river and cast his rod for trout, his movements as fluid and graceful as the icy waters singing over the boulders. The fisherman stood there, motionless, at home in this setting, quietly waiting for a tug on his line. The scene was hauntingly beautiful.

The man's patience reminded me of something. For a moment, I wasn't quite sure what. Then I remembered. I had noticed the same patience in every conversation I had had recently with park and tribal officials who have been working for decades to restore native salmon and steelhead runs to the Elwha. The stocks of Chinook, sockeye, coho, chum, and pink salmon, as well as steelhead, were once famous for their record-breaking size and numbers. They were the mainstay of the Lower Elwha Klallam tribal economy. Now salmon and steelhead have all but disappeared, impeded from spawning upstream by two turn-of-the-century dams built without the fish ladders required by the state.

"We must be patient. It's a long-term project, with good science and the 1992 Elwha River Ecosystem and Fisheries Restoration Act to back it up. It's up to Congress to allocate the funds to carry out the project now," said one park official. "If it doesn't happen in this generation, then it will happen in the next," said the Lower Elwha Klallam tribal representative. "We are in this for the long haul."

I was struck by their ability to see the big picture, by their concern for all parties involved. All were confident that funding hurdles would eventually be overcome once enough people realized what a win-win situation it is to buy and remove the old dam structures, allowing the river to return to its wild state and a functioning ecosystem that benefits all users of the river. What is remarkable is that most parties involved in this—public and private—agree. Now, there is cause for hope.

Tonight, sitting here under the forest canopy, as night falls over the river and all that is left is the soothing roar of water on rock, it's easy to believe in a kind of dynamic equilibrium, one that brings us to a point where we can make the right choices, if we are patient. And even as the thought comes to me, the fisherman begins to reel in his line, slowly, slowly, until a flash of silver illuminates the darkness.

Coho salmon leaping upstream in the Sol Duc River.

PAT O'HARA

The emerald clusters in the Olympic Peninsula's rocky tiara are its majestic temperate rain forests. Nourished by year-round rainfall, climax forests of shade-tolerant Sitka spruce, western hemlock, and western redcedar reach 30 stories high, 20 feet thick, and live centuries longer than sun-loving Douglas-fir, red alder, and other early pioneers. Assertive understory plants such as vine maple and devil's club all but conceal trilliums, oxalis, and other woodland neighbors. Shaggy redcedar, whose arrival 6,000 years ago boosted Northwest coastal Indian culture, is the helpful "spirit tree" of the forest. Big-leaf maple is a shapeshifter, bearded with spike moss and adorned with licorice fern and hundreds of different kinds of lichens. These harmless epiphytes absorb nutrients from moist air and contribute biomass and nitrogen to the forest. Competition for food and space is so fierce, in fact, that tree seedlings often root in spongey fallen trunks, where they form chorus lines of bandy-legged roots as ancient "nurse logs" disintegrate beneath them.

Big-leaf maples and red alders in the Queets Rain Forest, spring.

TERRY DONNELLY

Carpet of sword fern along the Hall of Mosses Trail, Hoh Rain Forest.

TERRY DONNELLY

The Bailey Range from Hurricane Ridge, sunset.   PAT O'HARA

The route to the high country passes through forested drainages. On the west side, rain forest changes to a predominantly western hemlock and silver fir mix at mid-elevation. The appearance of mountain hemlock forests leads the way into a diminishing tree zone characterized primarily by windblown dwarf *krummholz.* Inland, lowland forests outside Olympic National Park frequently contain fast-growing replanted Douglas-fir, joined by competing western hemlock. Above 3,500 feet, subalpine fir, mountain hemlock, and stands of lodgepole pine and long-lived Alaska yellow cedar mark the high country. This is a land isolated by blizzards and deep drifts for eight months of the year. Hurricane Ridge Road is intermittently plowed to provide access for sightseers, skiers, and snowshoers, but this is essentially a quiet time of year. Spring usually arrives in early June, when melting snow swells waterfalls and rivers, avalanche lilies appear in meadows, and a succession of lupine, asters, and other fast-bloomers carpet the swales.

Opposite: Ennis Creek, morning fog. STEVE TERRILL

FOR MORE INFORMATION

OLYMPIC NATIONAL PARK
  600 East Park Avenue
  Port Angeles, WA 98362
  (360) 452-4501

OLYMPIC NATIONAL PARK VISITOR CENTER
  3002 Mount Angeles Road
  Port Angeles, WA 98362
  (360) 452-0330

**VISIT THE NATIONAL PARKS ON
THE INTERNET:** http://www.nps.gov

ACCOMMODATIONS

INSIDE THE PARK:
KALALOCH LODGE
  (36 miles south of Forks)
  157151 Highway 101
  Forks, WA 98331
  (360) 962-2271, (360) 962-3391 (Fax)

LAKE CRESCENT LODGE
  416 Lake Crescent Road
  Port Angeles, WA 98363
  (360) 928-3211

LOG CABIN RESORT
  3183 E. Beach Road
  Port Angeles, WA 98363
  (360) 928-3325, (360) 928-2088 (Fax)

SOL DUC HOT SPRINGS RESORT
  PO Box 2169
  Port Angeles, WA 98362
  (360) 327-3583, (360) 327-3593 (Fax)

OUTSIDE THE PARK:
LAKE QUINAULT LODGE
  PO Box 7
  Lake Quinault, WA 98575
  (360) 288-2900, (360) 288-2901 (Fax)

NORTH OLYMPIC PENINSULA VISITOR & CONVENTION BUREAU
  (800) 942-4042

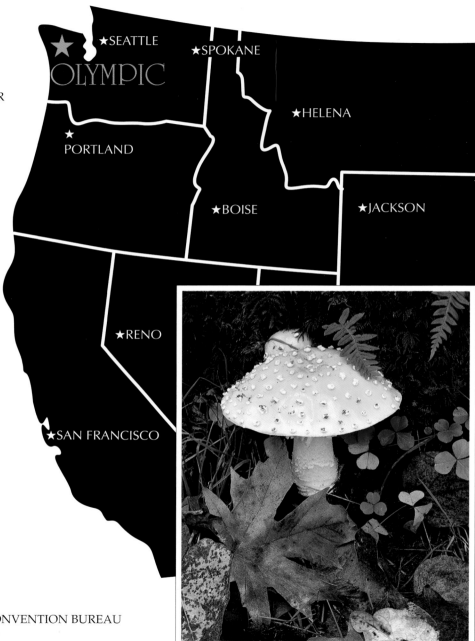

Mushrooms on the floor of Queets Rain Forest.   JEFF NICHOLAS